APPROVED

APPROVED

APPROVED

IN

IN

IN

OUT

OUT

OUT

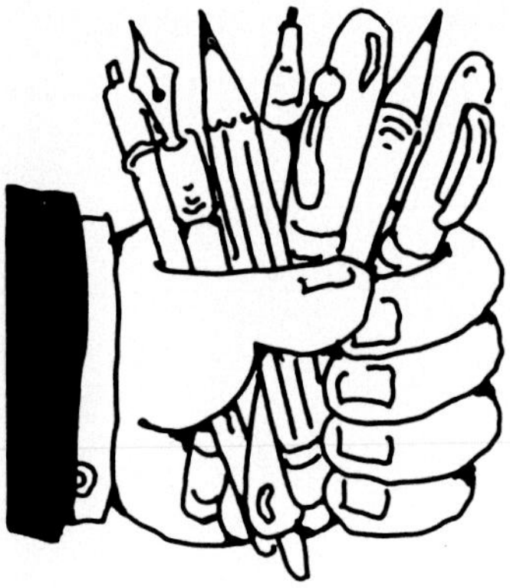

INK

EXPRESS MAIL

INK

EXPRESS MAIL

INK

EXPRESS MAIL

CAR PHONE

ANSWERING MACHINE

US
MAIL

CAR PHONE

ANSWERING MACHINE

US
MAIL

CAR PHONE

US
MAIL

ANSWERING MACHINE

EXPRESS MAIL

GLUE
LIQUID PAPER

SMOKING WORK AREA

EXPRESS MAIL

GLUE
LIQUID PAPER

SMOKING WORK AREA

EXPRESS MAIL

GLUE
LIQUID PAPER

SMOKING WORK AREA

BOSS
SALES KIT

NO SMOKING
WORK AREA

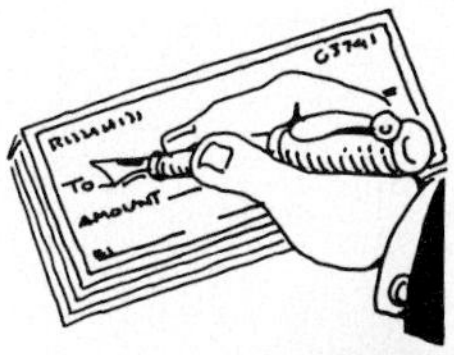
To
AMOUNT

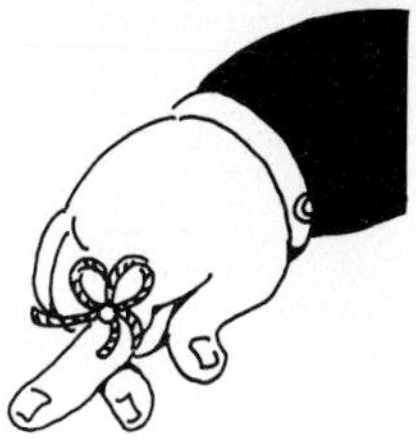

BOSS
SALES KIT

NO SMOKING
WORK AREA

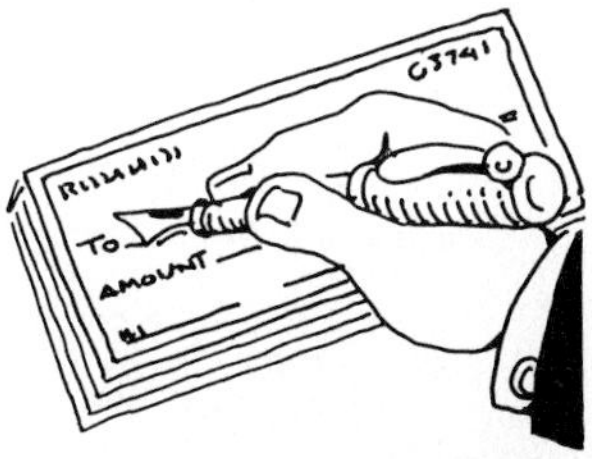
To
AMOUNT

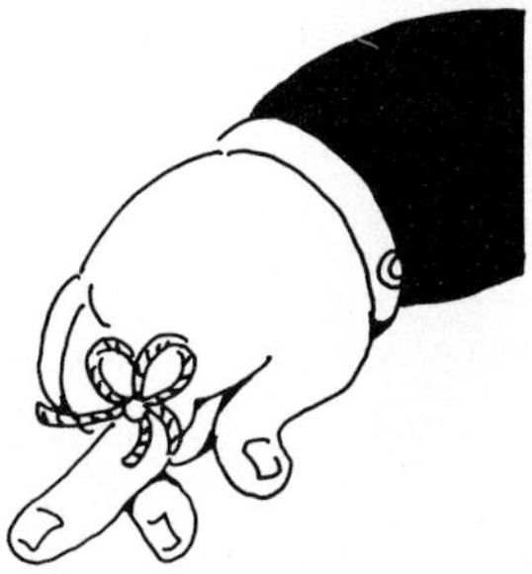

BOSS
SALES KIT

NO SMOKING
WORK AREA

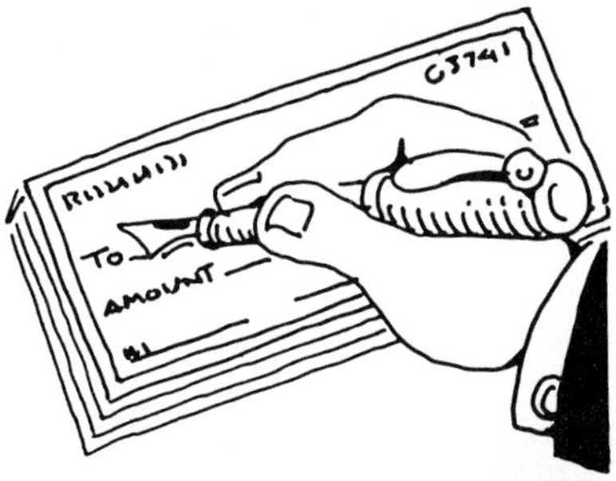
To
AMOUNT

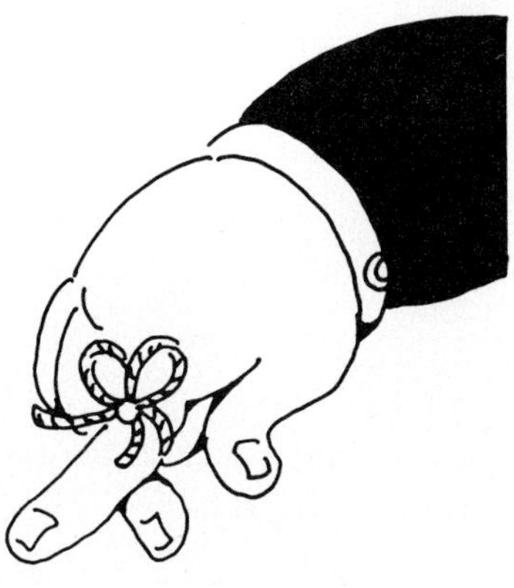

coffee

coffee

coffee

OUR CLIENT

OUR COMPETITOR

OUR CLIENT

OUR COMPETITOR

OUR CLIENT

OUR COMPETITOR

HELP WANTED

HELP WANTED

On Vacation

On Vacation

On Vacation

HELP WANTED

out to lunch

HELP WANTED

HELP WANTED

out to lunch

out to lunch

HELP WANTED

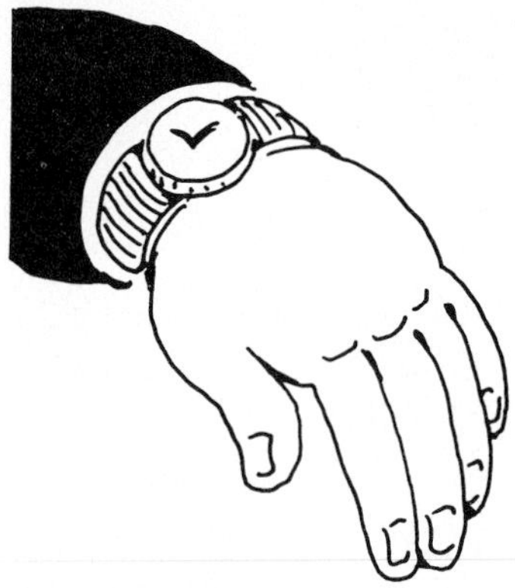

OFFICE
MOVERS

OFFICE
MOVERS

OFFICE
MOVERS

EMPLOYMENT AGENCY

EMPLOYMENT AGENCY

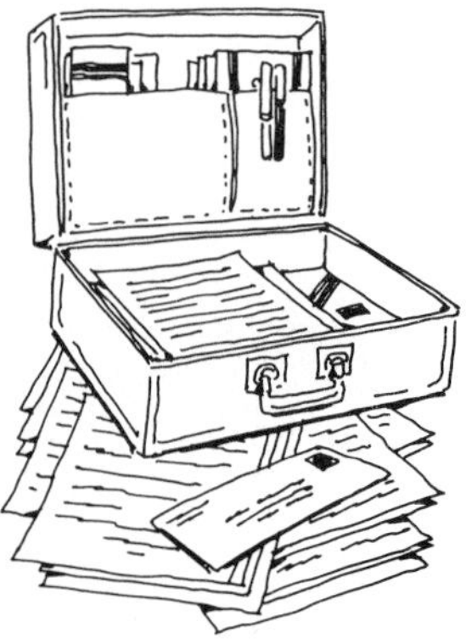

EMPLOYMENT AGENCY

RECEPTION

RECEPTION

RECEPTION

OFFICE SUPPLIES

OFFICE SUPPLIES

OFFICE SUPPLIES

RECEPTION

RECEPTION

RECEPTION

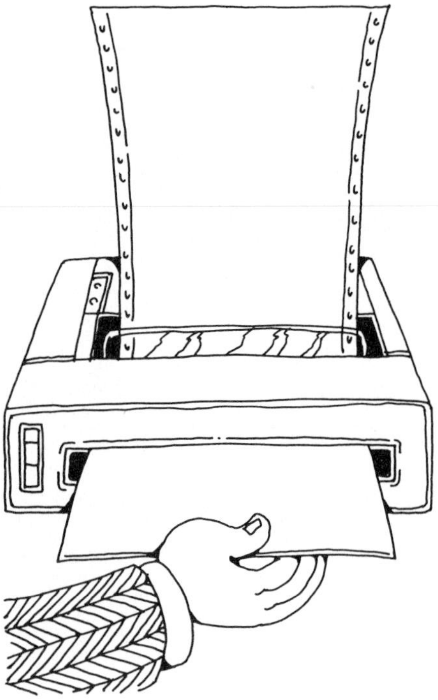
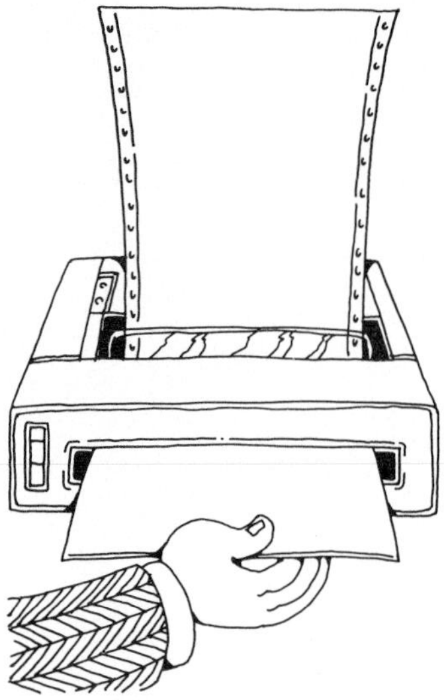

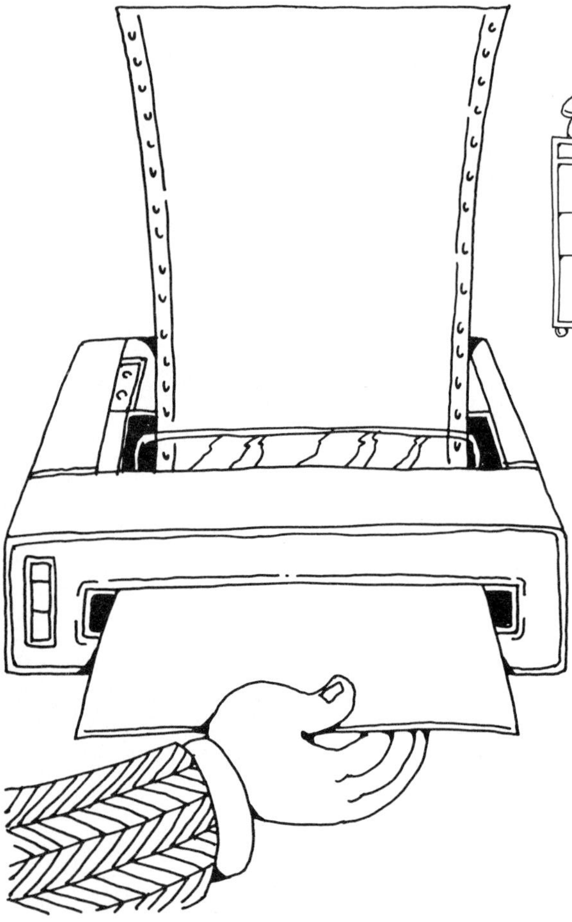

THE BOSS

RESUMÉ

THE BOSS

RESUME

THE BOSS

RESUME